TOMB TROUBLE

Contents

Haydn Middleton

Story illustrated by
Seb Burnett

Before Reading

Find out about

- How people in ancient Egypt tried to make dead bodies last forever – as MUMMIES!

Tricky words

- thousands
- ancient
- heart
- wrapped
- bandages
- buried
- tombs
- relatives

Introduce these tricky words and help the reader when they come across them later!

Text starter

The ancient Egyptians took 70 days to turn a dead body into a mummy. Then they buried the mummy in a stone tomb with treasure and food for the mummy to use in the next world.

Mummy Magic

A spooky box!

This box is thousands of years old.

It comes from ancient Egypt.

Once there was something spooky

inside it.

It was a dead body!
But it wasn't *just* a dead body.
Dead bodies rot and turn to dust.
In ancient Egypt, people wanted dead
bodies to last forever so they made the
dead body into a mummy.

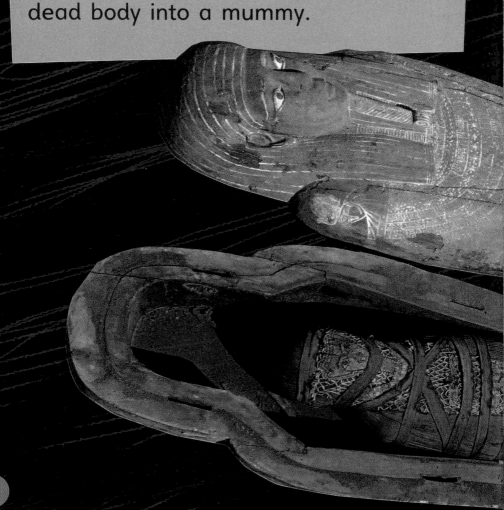

Why did they make mummies?

People in ancient Egypt thought that first you lived on Earth. But after you died, you went to live in *another* world. In this other world, you still needed your body.

That's why your body was turned into a mummy that never rotted.

How did they make mummies?

First, they made the dead body very dry. That stopped it from rotting. Then they had to take out most of the body's insides, but they left the heart. They pulled out the brain with a hook – through the nose.

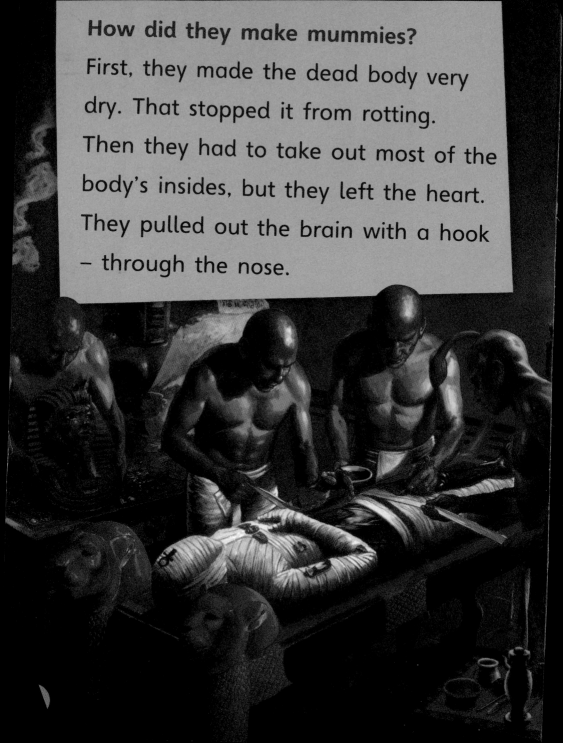

Then they wrapped the body in bandages to protect it. They used 20 layers of bandages!

It took 70 days to turn a dead body into a mummy. It was a very tricky job. They even turned dead pets into mummies too.

Crocodiles were also turned into mummies.

Lots of boxes

They put all the body's insides in painted jars. Then they put the mummy in a painted box.

If you were very rich, your painted box might be put inside another box and then that box would be put in another box!

Then the mummy box and jars were buried.

Mummies of kings and other rich people were buried in stone tombs. The biggest stone tombs of all were called pyramids.

Each tomb took over 20 years to build!

Inside the tombs

The stone tombs were full of treasure and food for the mummy – and even games to play!

There were tiny models of servants too. People hoped these models would come alive in the tomb to serve the mummy king!

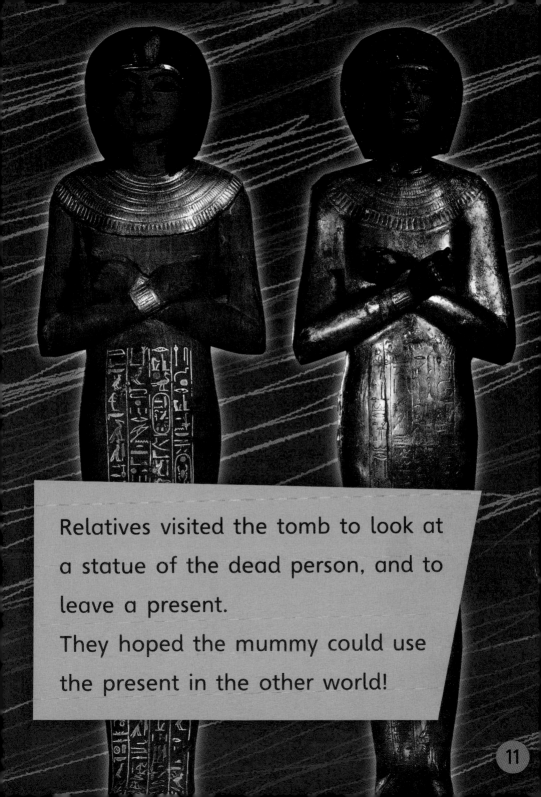

Relatives visited the tomb to look at a statue of the dead person, and to leave a present.

They hoped the mummy could use the present in the other world!

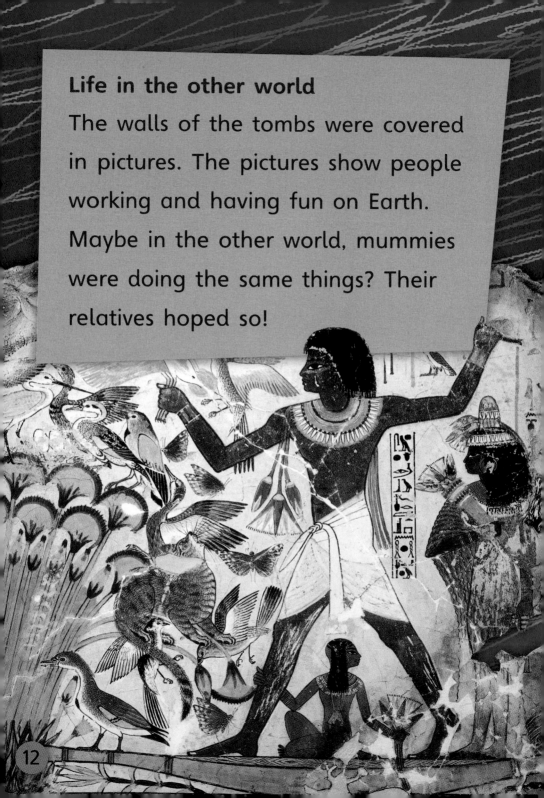

Life in the other world

The walls of the tombs were covered in pictures. The pictures show people working and having fun on Earth. Maybe in the other world, mummies were doing the same things? Their relatives hoped so!

But were mummies safe in the tombs?
No! Thieves often broke into the tombs
to steal treasure. Sometimes they took
the mummy as well. Why?
They turned the mummy into powder.
They said this powder was 'magic
medicine'. Spooky!

But what happened to the thieves? People thought the mummy would curse them. Then bad things would happen to them. Some mummies come back to life in this world just to get you. But that's only in horror films!

NEW THRILLS!
NEW TERROR!

LON CHANEY

The Mummy's Curse

PETER COE   KAY HARDING
MARTIN KOSLECK   VIRGINIA CHRISTINE
KURT KATCH

Text Detective

- Why did thieves break into the tombs?
- Would you like to be made into a mummy?

Word Detective

- **Phonic Focus:** Doubling consonants
  Page 6: What must be added to 'stop' before you can add 'ing'?
- Page 4: Find the plural of 'body'.
- Page 11: Find a word for 'family'.

Super Speller

Read these words:

mummy rotting stopped

Now try to spell them!

Q What music do mummies like most?

A Wrap music!

Before Reading

In this story

Schoolboy Mo who is also Mole Man

The Big Slug, his arch enemy

King Camel

Tricky words

- special
- ordinary
- Egypt
- pyramid
- terrible
- cinema
- stretched
- scared

> Introduce these tricky words and help the reader when they come across them later!

Story starter

Mo is no ordinary boy. He has a very special nose. When his nose smells trouble, something amazing happens – Mo turns into a super-hero called Mole Man! One day, the class is about to do a maths test when Mo smells bad trouble.

Mole Man at the Pyramids

Mo was sitting in class.

"Today," said the teacher, "we are having a maths test."

Just then, Mo's nose started twitching.

Mo had a special nose. He could smell trouble anywhere in the world. And he smelled *bad* trouble now. "Please can I go to the toilet?" asked Mo, and he ran off.

Mo rushed to his secret spot – and he burst out of his school clothes.

Mo was not an ordinary boy any more.
Mo was now ... **Mole Man!**
"Sniff, sniff," went Mole Man.
"Time to go digging."

So Mole Man set off underground
to find the trouble.
He dug faster than the speed of light!

Mole Man dug under land and sea. "I bet the Big Slug is behind this trouble," he said. "But Mole Man can sort it out."

Soon his nose was twitching really fast. "Sniff, sniff," went Mole Man.

"Time to tunnel *up*."

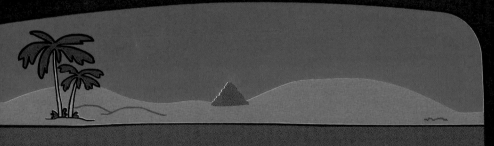

A moment later he burst up through the ground. He was in Egypt, next to the Pyramids.

"Mole Man!" cried King Camel. "You've come at just the right time! We're in terrible trouble. The Big Slug is going to steal a pyramid. He is going to turn it into the world's biggest 4-screen cinema – just for him."

"Sniff," went Mole Man. "I thought I smelled the Big Slug. But how is he going to steal the pyramid?"
Then Mole Man looked up.
There was the Big Slug. He was fixing a huge hook on to the pyramid.

"Quick," said Mole Man to King Camel.

"Tell all your camels to come here."

"*All* of them?" asked King Camel.

"All of them," said Mole Man.

King Camel roared – and a herd of camels came running.

"Excellent!" said Mole Man.

"Now what can we do?" asked King Camel.

"Tell all your camels to jump on the pyramid," said Mole Man.

What do you think Mole Man's plan is?

All the camels jumped on the pyramid. "Now the pyramid will be too heavy for the Big Slug to lift," said Mole Man.

But the Big Slug didn't see the camels.
"Lift!" shouted the Big Slug.
The rope stretched and stretched.
But the pyramid stayed on the ground.
"Higher!" screamed the Big Slug.

The Slugship went higher and higher. The rope stretched and stretched and then ... **SNAP!** The rope broke! The Slugship flew off but the pyramid was not on the end of the rope! "Come back!" screamed the Big Slug.

"This must be the work of Mole Man," shouted the Big Slug. "I'm coming to get you, Mole Man!"
But then he saw all the camels. They looked angry and the Big Slug was scared.

"Thanks for saving our pyramid,
Mole Man," said King Camel.
"No problem!" said Mole Man.
Then he dug all the way back to school
and changed into his school clothes.

Mo rushed back into class.

"Just in time," said his teacher.

"Where on Earth have you been?"

"Just to the Pyramids," said Mo.

His teacher smiled.

"You and your little stories," he said.

Quiz

Text Detective

- What was the Big Slug planning to turn the pyramid into?
- How do you think the Big Slug will get away from the camels?

Word Detective

- **Phonic Focus:** Doubling consonants
  Page 19: What must you add to 'dig' before you can add 'ing'?
- Page 19: Find a word made from two words.
- Page 29: Find a word meaning 'cross'.

Super Speller

Read these words:

running   quick   angry

Now try to spell them!

HA! HA! HA!

 What makes camels so grumpy?

They've always got the hump.

32